# COUNTDOWN

## ALL EYES ON GOD'S ULTIMATE ENDGAME

# JACK HIBBS

# CONTENTS

# INTRODUCTION

God's Word is the sure and firm foundation of all truth. And in this day and age, you and I need truth to make sure that we are on the straight and narrow path. The things that we're going to be looking at in this book are valuable for keeping us grounded and encouraged in our faith.

As we look around the world, we see things becoming more and more unstable. We see all eyes off of America as it quickly diminishes in power. We see all eyes on Israel, just as Bible prophecy foretold. And we also see that all over the world, all eyes are turning to God in these times of unprecedented uncertainty.

My friend, this is a good time to know the Bible. It is the Bible that will keep you from the error of the world's ways. It is the Bible that will shine light into the path of your life and lead you in the way of righteousness.

In this book, we will take a good look at what the Bible has to say about the times in which we are living, and what God has in store for the last days.

# CHAPTER
## ONE

————◦◦•◦◦————

The Deconstruction
of Morality

We are living in a culture that is declining morally, a world that is spiraling out of control as wickedness increases.

Two thousand years ago, Jesus said that there would come a time when deception would escalate. Matthew 24:3-5 records it. As you read it below, ask yourself if it's true about the age in which we live.

> *Now as [Jesus] sat on the Mount of Olives, the disciples came to Him privately, saying, "Tell us, when will these things be? And what will be the sign of Your coming, and of the end of the age?"*

> *And Jesus answered and said to them: "Take heed that no one deceives you. For many will come in My name, saying, 'I am the Christ,' and will deceive many.*

## THINGS ARE ESCALATING

An **escalation of deception** is what Jesus predicted would come. In addition, He told us that there would be an **escalation of calamities on the earth.**

> *And there will be famines, pestilences, and earthquakes in various places.* (Matthew 24:7)

He also warned there would be **an escalation of offense, betrayal, and hatred** among humankind.

> *Then many will be offended, will betray one another, and will hate one another.* (Matthew 24:10)

Is that true of our modern culture? Do you see the escalation of those things happening in the world today?

We know that there will also come a time of **escalation regarding the devaluing of human life** and an **escalation of disregard for law.** In Luke 17:26-30, He said,

> As it was in the days of Noah, so it will be also in the days of the Son of Man: They ate, they drank, they married wives, they were given in marriage, until the day that Noah entered the ark, and the flood came and destroyed them all. Likewise as it was also in the days of Lot: They ate, they drank, they bought, they sold, they planted, they built; but on the day that Lot went out of Sodom it rained fire and brimstone from heaven and destroyed them all. Even so will it be in the day when the Son of Man is revealed.

This passage says that in the last days it will be like it was in the days of Noah. How were things in the days of Noah? Genesis 6:5 tells us:

> The Lord saw that the wickedness of man was great in the earth, and that every intent of the thoughts of his heart was only evil continually.

Sound familiar?

What else did Jesus say would escalate?

There will come an **escalation of war and threats**—saber-rattling all around the world.

> "And you will hear of wars and rumors of wars" (Matthew 24:6).

There will be an **escalation of racism** upon the earth. Matthew 24:7 says,

> *"For nation will rise against nation."*

The word used for *nation* here is *ethnos*. "*Ethnos* will rise against *ethnos*." There'll be race wars in the earth. We're seeing that right now on a global scale for the first time in all of human history. How do you explain that?

An **escalation of geopolitical tension** is coming:

> *"Kingdom against kingdom."* (Matthew 24:7)

Political powers will attack political powers, and we see that today on a worldwide scale as well. In fact, in the last century, the world for the first time in global history hosted at least two world wars. I say "at least two" because many would consider the war on terrorism as a third world war.

There will also come **escalation of fear and the supernatural.**

> *"There will be fearful sights and great signs from heaven."* (Luke 21:11)

In this instance, the word *heaven* is not referring to heaven where God is, but in the observable sky. I don't believe in aliens or little green men flying around with spaceships. However, I believe in all of the hype that goes on regarding aliens.

"But don't you believe that something crashed in Roswell?"

I've never seen it, but let's say it did. If something crashed in Roswell, it's of demonic origin.

Does that sound like the latest Hollywood sci-fi blockbuster?

Demonic. I don't believe in visitors from other planets. I believe in visitors from hell. They're called demons. Jesus spoke about them, and they're fallen angels.

If something takes you away from Jesus and from the security of the Word of God, then it's demonic.

Then, finally, the Bible says there will come a great **escalation of the divorce of man from God**. God's Word predicted that man would distance himself from God and stand in opposition to all things concerning God—and we have. We remove God from our classrooms, from our courts, from our marriages. We pretend God is no longer something we have to deal with or factor into our thinking. We've become our own gods. *We* will call the shots. *We* will run the show.

What happens to a culture when that takes place?

Whenever man puts himself in control, whenever we have the opportunity to be, as it were, our own gods with power, with law, and with influence, we might start out with good intentions—but remember the old saying: "Power corrupts, but absolute power corrupts absolutely." We simply can't handle it.

I spoke to some young pastors recently, and I mentioned to them, "You need to be careful because in your lives, God wants to use you, and your greatest danger is not defeat. Your greatest danger is not setbacks and trials. Your greatest danger is success." Do you want to destroy somebody? Elevate them too quickly. Human beings simply can't handle it.

# MORALITY IS DISINTEGRATING

There is a deconstruction of morality that is underway.

*Morality* is a word that people don't like to hear. They see it as a synonym for constraint, limitation, or restriction of freedom. But morality is simply knowing what is right or wrong and behaving accordingly.

According to God's Word, there's going to be a deconstruction of morality in the last days. Look at Romans 1:26:

> *For this reason God gave them up to vile passions...*

That phrase "for this reason" gives the indication that it's something that God was forced to do. It's not the way He would have wished it to be, but mankind gave Him reason to give them up to their vile passions. What was that reason? It's found in the prior verse:

> *[They] exchanged the truth of God for the lie, and worshiped and served the creature rather than the Creator.* (Romans 1:25)

Our deconstruction of morality has forced God's hand.

You need to remember that God is not willing that anyone should perish. God is reaching out, God is calling out, and God is crying out, extending salvation and hope. But "for this reason," He gives them up. It's a statement of fact, based on our actions. He's responding with His judgment "for this reason."

# WHEN GOD ACQUIESCES

That phrase "gave them up" gives the idea of handing them

over. He hands them over to what they ultimately want. That's terrifying!

Picture a small child nagging his mom. "Mommy, can I have a cookie? I want a cookie. Mommy, please. I want a cookie. I want a cookie. Cookie, cookie, cookie, cookie, cookie." And of course the mom is on the phone, baking a cake, selling things on Etsy, mowing the lawn, and vacuuming—all simultaneously. She's got a baby on her hip and the other one is pulling at her, whining: "Cookie, cookie, cookie, cookie..."

In a moment of desperation, she just grabs the whole package of cookies and just gives it to him. "Here. You want cookies? Here's your cookies," and she hands over the cookies to shut the kid up. "Here, eat the cookies."

That might not be the best illustration because God is never too busy for us and never gets frustrated with us, but it's the idea of giving them over to their own passions. We say, "I want this. I want this. I want this."

God says, "It's not good for you. It's not good for you. It's not good for you."

"I want it. I want it. I want it."

Finally, it comes to a point when God says, "You're never going to get off of this desire of yours, this passion that is consuming you. Here it is. You want it? You can have it."

Do you remember the account of the children of Israel wandering around the wilderness and complaining? "Manna—we're sick of it!"

Every day, they'd wake up in the morning, and the Bible says

God would provide them with manna. It would just appear for them to eat. It was a divine act of God that food would be there each day on the ground in front of them—a delivery service so efficient it would put Amazon right out of business. The Bible says they would wake up and it would be right outside their tent door. They didn't have to shop for it or prepare it or cook it— they could just eat it. It was right there at their fingertips.

Despite that, they complained: "We're sick of this stuff. We want something different. Oh, I wish we were back in Egypt where they had onions." That's what they said! "Remember those leeks and onions?"

They whined about it so much, God told Moses, "You know what? About this time tomorrow, I'm going to cause a wind to blow, and quail are going to come flying by in the wind."

So the wind blows, and all these quail come flying through, and everybody is just grabbing quail by their little necks and feet. And the people eat so much quail it's practically coming out of their noses. But the Bible says,

> He gave them their request,
> But sent leanness into their soul. (Psalm 106:15)

They became carnal.

What's the moral of the teaching? If what you want is against what God wants, but you keep harping on it, eventually you'll probably get it. When you get it, it will be your demise, and you'll have no one to blame but yourself.

# VILE PASSIONS

God gave them up to their vile passions. That word *vile* means to use something in an uncommon or improper way. It speaks of something shameful, repulsive, or wrong.

I recently saw a school flyer targeted for teenagers. It said "Teens! Your health is in your hands!" Then it listed the following:

* Teen pregnancy prevention
* Birth control
* Condoms
* Emergency contraception
* STI and HIV testing
* Pregnancy testing
* Sexual health education

Instead of approaching the topic of sex from a biblical perspective, our culture is insistent on following its own vile passions—and even encouraging our kids to misuse it in an improper way.

There is a degradation, a disintegration, a decomposition of morality in our world today, and we can plainly see that the rate of this downfall is increasing exponentially with each passing day.

This wickedness that we are seeing is one of the signs that we are accelerating toward the end times faster than we have ever been before.

Luke 21:28 tells us,

> *Now when these things begin to happen, look up and lift up your heads, because your redemption draws near.*

We need to look up! In other words, all eyes on God!

# CHAPTER
## TWO

———•———

## All Eyes on God

Before we get into some of the indicators we're seeing that fall in line with end-times prophecy, I want to give you some encouragement. That's what Jesus did in John 14:1, where He said:

> Let not your heart be troubled; you believe in God, believe also in Me.

When we look around our troubling world, we do not have to be troubled. In fact, as we examine these topics in this book, we should actually be excited. Regarding what's coming in the future, you can either get run over by it, or you can understand that God has revealed these things to give us assurance, and we can therefore find joy in the fact that He holds the events of the future in His hands.

Before we dive in, here are some preparatory verses for context:

In Luke 21:36 (NIV), Jesus says to us,

> Be always on the watch, and pray that you may be able to escape all that is about to happen, and that you may be able to stand before the Son of Man.

Titus 2:12-13 tells us,

> We should live soberly, righteously, and godly in the present age, looking for the blessed hope and glorious appearing of our great God and Savior Jesus Christ.

Every believer should be on the watch—looking, scanning, observing the horizon for "the blessed hope and the glorious appearing of our great God and Savior." This isn't a casual looking, but an expectant and eager anticipation.

In a later chapter, we will take a close look at this glorious appearing, an event we call the Rapture.

# THE CHESS PIECES ARE MOVING

In our current global situation, we see an awakening taking place. When I say "awakening," I don't mean just spiritually. I'm also talking about events and key players in end-times prophecy.

Iran—referred to in the Bible as Persia—is awakening. China is awakening. North Korea is awakening. Russia is awakening. For the last several years these players have been, by and large, contained. But things have changed. Pieces on the board are moving.

Recent war between Russia and Ukraine is evidence that Russia has been emboldened to move in more aggressive ways. As world leaders cower before this bully, and there is no longer a strong arm to hold it in check, Russia finds itself in a golden moment to make a move. I encourage you to keep your eyes on other players: Cuba, Venezuela, North Korea. Keep your eyes on Taiwan and on the areas of Syria and Lebanon. Keep your eyes on the Northeastern regions of the Mediterranean up toward the Black Sea.

Why do I tell you to watch these things? Because they could lead to the events prophesied in Ezekiel 38. I've been a Christian for over 46 years, and I can honestly say that the world has never been this well aligned to fulfill Ezekiel 38 than it is at this very time.

So what does Ezekiel 38 tell us? Let's look at it:

> Now the word of the Lord came to me, saying, "Son of man, set your face against Gog, of the land of Magog, the prince of Rosh, Meshech, and Tubal, and prophesy against him, and say, 'Thus says the Lord God: "Behold, I

*am against you, O Gog, the prince of Rosh, Meshech, and Tubal."* (Verses 1-3)

*Gog* is a title that denotes both a military leader and a political leader in one person—a warlord politician. And the land of Rosh is the northern region above the Caucasus Mountains—what is today the land of Russia. Ezekiel continues God's prophecy to this leader, saying,

> *"I will turn you around, put hooks into your jaws, and lead you out, with all your army, horses, and horsemen, all splendidly clothed, a great company with bucklers and shields, all of them handling swords. Persia, Ethiopia, and Libya are with them, all of them with shield and helmet; Gomer and all its troops; the house of Togarmah from the far north and all its troops—many people are with you."* (Verses 4-6)

These names refer to the countries that will ally themselves with Russia to come against Israel, an event we read about in the following verses. The Lord tells Gog,

> *"In the latter years you will come into the land of those brought back from the sword and gathered from many people on the mountains of Israel, which had long been desolate; they were brought out of the nations, and now all of them dwell safely. You will ascend, coming like a storm, covering the land like a cloud, you and all your troops and many peoples with you."* (Verses 8-9)

This alliance will set itself up against Israel and attack them like a storm.

> *"Thus says the Lord God: 'On that day it shall come to pass that thoughts will arise in your mind, and you will make an evil plan: You will say, "I will go up against a land of unwalled villages; I will go to a peaceful people, who dwell safely, all of them dwelling without walls, and having neither bars nor gates"—to take plunder and to take booty, to stretch out your hand against the waste places that are again inhabited, and against a people gathered from the nations, who have acquired livestock and goods, who dwell in the midst of the land.'"* (Verses 10-12)

Notice that God calls this an "*evil plan,*" an unprovoked attack on a peaceful people. He continues:

> *"Sheba, Dedan, the merchants of Tarshish, and all their young lions will say to you, 'Have you come to take plunder? Have you gathered your army to take booty, to carry away silver and gold, to take away livestock and goods, to take great plunder?'"* (Verse 13)

Sheba and Dedan refer to the area of Saudi Arabia, which is currently on good terms with Israel. Notice in this prophecy, they are not attacking Israel, but are essentially saying to Israel's attackers, "Why are you doing this?" The same goes for "*the merchants of Tarshish,*" indicating the area of Portugal and Spain.

> *"Therefore, son of man, prophesy and say to Gog, 'Thus says the Lord God: "On that day when My people Israel dwell safely, will you not know it? Then you will come from your place out of the far north, you and many peoples with you, all of them riding on horses, a great company and a mighty army. You will come up against My people Israel like a cloud, to cover the land. It will be*

*in the latter days that I will bring you against My land, so that the nations may know Me, when I am hallowed in you, O Gog, before their eyes."* (Verses 14-17)

When is this to happen? "*In the latter days.*" And one of the results of this attack is that the world's attention will be drawn to the Lord.

*"And it will come to pass at the same time, when Gog comes against the land of Israel," says the Lord God, "that My fury will show in My face. For in My jealousy and in the fire of My wrath I have spoken: 'Surely in that day there shall be a great earthquake in the land of Israel, so that the fish of the sea, the birds of the heavens, the beasts of the field, all creeping things that creep on the earth, and all men who are on the face of the earth shall shake at My presence. The mountains shall be thrown down, the steep places shall fall, and every wall shall fall to the ground.' I will call for a sword against Gog throughout all My mountains," says the Lord God.* (Verses 18-21)

The outcome of this conflict is not good for Gog and his allies. In fact,

*"I will bring him to judgment with pestilence and bloodshed; I will rain down on him, on his troops, and on the many peoples who are with him, flooding rain, great hailstones, fire, and brimstone. Thus I will magnify Myself and sanctify Myself, and I will be known in the eyes of many nations. Then they shall know that I am the Lord."'* (Verses 22-23)

Bible scholars agree that this failed attack by Russia and its allies as outlined in Ezekiel 38 will take place either just before the Rapture of the Church, or just after it.

And as we look at these Scriptures in light of all that's going on, we can see how the conditions are ripe for their fulfillment. We're seeing saber-rattling. We're seeing an awakening, all of a sudden, of nations. And there's been a bizarre global shift among the world's power players.

Like lions backed into a corner by a lion tamer, these nations were previously held in place. They weren't happy about it, but they were held in check. And then, all of a sudden, things have been shaken. I'm not talking about politics. I'm talking about the hand of God.

Right now, all eyes are on God.

What do I mean by that? People are awakening, and they're asking questions about God and about the end of the world. People are jarred. They are reading headlines and watching news clips that have them thinking about what's going to happen in the future. God says in Isaiah 45:21,

> *Who has declared this from ancient time?*
> *Who has told it from that time?*
> *Have not I, the Lord?*
> *And there is no other God besides Me,*
> *A just God and a Savior;*
> *There is none besides Me.*

Our God is the only one who can accurately predict the future. And this is what He says in the verse that follows:

> *Look to Me, and be saved,*
> *All you ends of the earth!*
> *For I am God, and there is no other.* (Isaiah 45:22)

In the midst of all the shaking and the posturing, it's God's will right now that the world would wake up to these things and understand that He's in control. He knows exactly what's going on.

We are living in an unprecedented time, and it's been said, both in our nation and around the world, that there's likely no return to "normal." The uncertainty and chaos is likely to remain. Nobody wants to hear that, but it's very believable, isn't it?

As a result, people are beginning to question everything. And so they should. People are unsettled. People are looking for answers.

And that's what I mean when I say that all eyes are upon God.

## UNSHAKEABLE

In Haggai 2:6, we read,

> *This is what the Lord Almighty says: 'In a little while I will once more shake the heavens and the earth, the sea and the dry land.*

Listen, He's not poetically speaking here. This is not God writing a play. He means it. He is going to shake things up.

In verse 7, God goes on to say,

> *I will shake all nations, and what is desired by all nations will come, and I will fill this house* [speaking of His temple] *with glory,' says the Lord Almighty.*

God is going to shake the nations, and He is going to fill His house with glory. God knows what's going on in the Church. And there's a healthy and much-needed division taking place within the Church as a result of these unprecedented times. This division is increasing every week. I see this division as a sifting of true believers.

But we need to remember that in Hebrews 12:28, the Bible says,

> *Therefore, since we are receiving a kingdom which cannot be shaken, let us have grace, by which we may serve God acceptably with reverence and godly fear.*

If you are a true follower of Christ, then you are part of a kingdom that cannot be shaken.

What are we to do, knowing that God's kingdom cannot be shaken? Look at Hebrews again:

> *Therefore, since we are receiving a kingdom which cannot be shaken, let us have grace, by which we may serve God acceptably with reverence and godly fear.*

Godly fear is an awesome thing. Another way to say it is "godly awe." Why are we to have godly fear? Because our God is a consuming fire. It's the will of God that we reverently come to the saving, loving, and forgiving knowledge of Jesus Christ in order that He would become our Lord and Savior.

# GOD IS GETTING PEOPLE'S ATTENTION

The urgency of God's Word now is not like it has been at any other time in recent history. For you and me to be equipped right now as believers is so very important. Jesus announced 2,000 years ago that the fields are white unto harvest (John 4:35). What Jesus was telling us by that statement is that people need the Lord. People need the hope of the Bible and the assurance of truth. Jesus was speaking about souls being ready to receive truth.

That's where you and I come in as followers of Jesus Christ in an unstable time. In this world that we are living in, people are questioning: "What is it that I believe in? Is it firm? Is it steadfast? Is it true?" God's truth wonderfully answers those questions.

Yes, more than ever, it's all eyes on God.

People are turning to the Bible all over the world. In fact, recently we heard news from the State Department indicating that according to their data, more people were downloading the Bible in the year 2020 than ever before. Shaken by COVID and the uncertainty of unprecedented worldwide panic, they wanted to find out what God's Word says. These downloads were largely happening in many countries where the gospel has been banished. What does that mean? It means those individuals are looking for truth.

And how about you? More than ever, you and I need the truth of God's Word to be active in our lives, to bring us peace. We must understand that God gave us Bible prophecy to prepare us for these times. God's Word in our lives also serves to energize you and me to tell the world about the love of God. That's so incredibly important.

The eyes of people all over the world are focusing on God. Are yours?

And then again you'd allow the shrieking ... loose the head
As we go over the ... ... ... ... ... ... ... ... ...
... ... ... ... ... ... ...
... ... ... ... ... ... ... ... ...
... ... ... ... ... ... ... ... ... ... ...
... ... ...

... ... ... ... ... ... ... ... ... ...

# CHAPTER
## THREE

---

## All Eyes Off America

If you live in the United States, you live in a country that, in many ways, considers God as just a really big American.

But according to Scripture, America is not even depicted in Bible prophecy. How could the greatest nation that has ever graced this planet not be listed as a major player in end-time events? By the way, that designation, "the greatest nation on earth," isn't just a patriotic nickname. American exceptionalism stems from the fact that the United States has the greatest economy, the strongest military, the most exceptional freedoms, the greatest inventions, and the most transcendent constitution that a governed people have ever experienced.

And yet, where is America in Bible prophecy? It's a sobering question.

One of our national mottos is "In God We Trust," but that is no longer the case. And as a result, we're going to see in this chapter that you and I are living at a time where all eyes are off America.

It pains me to say it, and it probably pains you to read it, but America is drifting from its prominence on the world scene.

We are a nation that was founded on biblical principles, but we as a culture have, by and large, forgotten and rejected that history and turned away from those principles. As a result, we're hanging on to the truth of God's Word in this nation by a thread. And if we let that go, then there's nothing else left.

Yes, we are still hanging on to this truth, however precariously it may be, and it is my prayer that before we are completely lost, God would send a revival to America. Without God moving to bring about revival, there's no hope for America. We have cut ties with our ancient foundations, and we need to get back to God. We need to get back to His Word.

## AMERICA IN DECLINE

There has never been a time like you and I are living in right now. Our nation has gone from the pinnacle of success and freedom to a place of crippling fear, debilitating confusion, and lost liberties. It's as though we were invaded by a foreign army. We have surrendered. We have given up at the first smell of battle. We've folded. We've failed to discern the times and the seasons in which we live. Our nation is gasping for air, and America as we knew it is no more.

According to Bible teaching and prophecy, America must go away. Did you know that America cannot stand as we've known it? America is, at this moment, leaderless. National policy has been exchanged for socialism, so-called "human rights," and the liberal agenda. The Constitution is now being declared a living document so that it can be changed at a whim.

## AMERICA NO LONGER KNOWS GOD

If someone says, "God bless America," our response could easily be, "What God are you talking about?" A recent public prayer given to open Congress ended with this phrase:

> "We ask it in the name of the monotheistic God, Brahma, and God known by many names by many different faiths. Amen and A-woman."

First of all, "the monotheistic God" is the God of the Bible. His name is Yah or Yahweh or Jehovah.

But the Congressman who spoke this prayer committed a high-handed treasonous act against the God of heaven by calling the monotheistic God of the Bible "Brahma." Brahma is one of the many gods of Hinduism. It is a theological impossibility to attempt to meld Brahma with the God that you and I know. Hinduism is not monotheistic. Brahma is not Jehovah. Brahma is not Yah of the Bible.

The Bible says that it is at the name of Jesus that every knee will bow and every tongue will confess that Jesus Christ is Lord, to the glory of God the Father.

All eyes are off America because America has jettisoned God for decades. As a result of our pushing Him out, God has left the building. He's gone. "Ichabod," which means "the glory of the Lord has departed," is written across our nation.

When our government says, "In God we trust," I don't know who they're talking about anymore. Apparently, Brahma is the current God that will be presiding over and protecting America during the current governmental administration. Brahma is a hand-crafted idol that doesn't have an ounce of power. How is it going to protect and provide for America?

Yet the God of the Bible is omnipotent, omnipresent, and omniscient.

Perhaps you think that I'm being too harsh in my assessment of America's government and its current spiritual status. If so, then let me ask you this: Do our leaders today approve of us praying publicly in the name of Jesus? No. Do our current leaders allow us to speak freely, preach, and teach the Bible without censorship? No.

On the whole, America has become antagonistic to the one true God.

## CENSORSHIP IN AMERICA

There are a handful of men who are basically running the social media world, and they are censoring anything that isn't acceptable to their opinions. They have the power to shut down any voice around the world that says anything contrary to their agenda.

I quit Twitter a while ago (I would have eventually been thrown off anyway), and I didn't expect to have anything more to do with it. But then someone recreated an account to be like mine and pretended to be me. This imposter is ripping off thousands of people all over the globe and saying all kinds of things in my name. They've taken my pictures and mimicked my posts and it's hard for some people to tell that it isn't me.

When we raised the issue to Twitter, their response was, "We don't edit parody." They've concluded that this person mimicking me is just a form of parody and they've told me they are not going to remove it. People are commenting on the imposter's posts, saying, "Jack, I can't believe you said that," and I have no way of commenting back. This guy pretends to be me and speaks in my voice and Twitter says, "That's just fine with us."

There is a censorship and a silencing and a twisting of communication that is happening in America, and especially regarding the truths found in the Bible.

But Psalm 2:4-5 says,

> *He who sits in the heavens shall laugh;*
> *The Lord shall hold them in derision.*
> *Then He shall speak to them in His wrath,*
> *And distress them in His deep displeasure.*

God's not happy. That's why I believe judgment is coming. God owes the nations judgment, and that includes America.

Persecution is coming. It's already started. Your first amendment rights are already deteriorating. But persecution will not stop Christians from preaching the gospel. And here's something to remember and look for: persecution always backfires because under the pressure of persecution, salvation sweeps cities, counties, states, and nations.

I saw a headline before COVID that said, "The US Decline of Christianity Continues at Rapid Pace" and the article had all sorts of Pew research analysis. But since that time, I've seen a different trend. When the Word of God is being taught and not apologized for at church—when people are given the opportunity to be adults and live their life in the fear of God rather than the fear of government—that church explodes. There's a revival taking place among those where the Bible is being proclaimed, and God is on the move.

Listen, you and I may not have America anymore, but we've got Jesus Christ.

# WILL WE SEE REVIVAL IN AMERICA?

As a nation, we need to get back to God. Is that going to happen? I don't know. I pray it does. I don't know what's going on in our country. Don't be fooled. Nobody else knows either.

The decline of Christianity in the United States continues at a rapid pace. Membership from Baptist, Southern Baptist, Lutheran, Methodist, Catholic, Assembly of God, Presbyterian, and other denominations—they are all going down. They're all losing people. That doesn't bother me. Don't let that bother you. That's not necessarily a bad thing, because so many of those entities have almost fully departed from the authoritative Word of God. They've walked away from or neglected the truths of the Bible.

And God is saying to some of the individuals and congregations in those denominations, "Hey, come out and be separate from them." Can you believe that He does that? In 2 Corinthians 6:17 and Revelation 18:4, God essentially tells His people, "Come out from among them." Don't hang out in a false church where Christ is not glorified, where His Word is not taught, and where you're not trained in the things of God so that you might go out into the world and make a difference.

Church is not a club. It's not to meet any standards that the world sets as to what is acceptable and not acceptable. The Church is a living, breathing entity given to us from heaven. It was created by the Holy Spirit. It was bought by the blood of Christ. It doesn't need to meet earthly or governmental requirements. It is the Church of the living God.

You can easily envision, in our age, how the Church will be pitted against godless governments and godless leaders. We're rapidly moving toward that, even now.

# LIVING IN A GODLESS AMERICA

So with all that we're hearing about and all that we're seeing in our culture today, what are we to do?

1) We trust God, because God is trustworthy. The reality that God exists and heaven is real transcends anything that a national government might tell us. I am delighted that the Bible tells us that those of us who trust Christ have a citizenship that is established in heaven.

2) We pray for America. We should absolutely be praying for revival and renewal.

3) We let our voice be heard about what is right, and we stand up against what's wrong. According to a biblical worldview, we're commanded to do that.

I want to encourage you to live boldly for Jesus. God has told us in various places throughout Scripture that we are luminaries of truth. Jesus said, in Matthew's Gospel,

> Let your light so shine before men, that they may see your good works and glorify your Father in heaven.
> (Matthew 5:16)

That statement implies that we, as believers, are going to be encountering dark days. In these dark days that we find ourselves in, let the truth of God's Word shine out of you. That means, what you and I are to promote is not our feelings and not our opinions, but as God's ambassadors, we are to promote God's truth in the ever-darkening world around us.

In Luke 12, Jesus taught us that we need to be very wise about having our lamps burning in this dark time. Jesus used an everyday image for the people of Israel at that time. They would use lamps that burned oil, and it was prudent to have enough oil on hand to keep their lamps always burning, especially as it began to grow dark. In the same way, we should be prepared. The Bible also makes it very clear that the presence of oil is symbolic of the presence of the Holy Spirit in the life of a believer. So more than ever, you and I need to be in the Word of God, putting what we read into practice, with the guidance of the Holy Spirit.

Obedience is doing what we have been instructed to do, and we must make the intentional decision to do what we have learned. Jesus said,

> *"Why do you call Me 'Lord, Lord,' and not do the things which I say?"* (Luke 6:46)

The Bible tells us that we ought to be doers of the Word and not hearers only. At this time in our nation's history, we need to know what God's Word says and then do it. We don't need another sermon unless we're going to put into practice the things we are learning. We don't want to be people who go to church on Sunday and then don't think about God again until the next Sunday rolls around. That's not following Christ. It's not what God wants from us.

More than ever, let's stop being spectators to Christianity. Real and practical Christianity is the Holy Spirit doing His will in your life. Christianity is not what you and I can muster up enough strength to do. It's not us determining that we're going to do this, that, or the other. No, Christianity is knowing what God's Word says and letting God do His work through us. Christianity is us being like Jesus in the world around us.

The hour is late. Christ is coming back. Look around at this world. There are indicators everywhere that His return is imminent. So what are we supposed to do? We are to live like Jesus. How do we do that? We are to know His Word and then put it into action. Christianity, when lived out biblically, should be the most exciting, loving, truth-filled life that you can experience in this world. I hope that's the life you're living.

# CHAPTER
## FOUR

All Eyes on Israel

Ezekiel tells us that one of the indicators of the end times would be that Israel would become a nation again. Isaiah said the same thing—that one of the timestamp indicators of God's return would be the people of Israel going back into their land, and Jerusalem becoming its capital.

You and I are living right now in a time when that has come about.

What's so comforting is that we worship a God who knows the future. When you and I pick up our Bibles, we're not picking up some old dusty book. We're picking up prophecies that are timelier and more relevant than today's newspaper.

## BIBLE PROPHECY MATTERS

My friend, Bible prophecy matters. So when God's Word speaks about times and events and happenings, we want to pay close attention. God gives us insight into these things that we might be people who are at peace because we know what's coming. We don't have to worry and bite our nails like the rest of the world.

Especially in times like these, God wants to communicate to you His truth. And you need to make a decision about what you're going to listen to.

Look at it this way. If you have been in war or combat, you know that one of the first things that you do is gather intel for the mission. And one of the first strategies you employ is figuring out how to take out the enemy's communications.

I don't care how big the army is. I don't care how big the nation is. If you want to gain the upper hand, you take out communications. By the way, the United States is really good at that. As a nation, as a war machine, we usually go in a few days in advance and knock out the enemy's communication systems by stealth, or even remotely.

Here's the point I am making: when communication is not clear, people get confused. That's what happens in war. And you and I right now are at war. Not a war for any territory. Not for any loot or glory or land. We are at war for souls. That's what we're fighting for. You and I, as believers, we're living for the souls of men and women and boys and girls.

The Bible says that we are Jesus' ambassadors. As believers, we're deployed all around the world. We're trying to share the gospel with people. We're trying to communicate the truth. And the enemy wants to mess that up constantly with false teaching, false prophets, false faith, and to confuse people's ability to come to the knowledge that Jesus is the way, the truth, and the life. The enemy hates that Jesus died on the cross for our sins to set us free, and he will do everything in his power to prevent the communication of that message.

That's why he floods the scene with allurements and lust and pride and desire. Those are not cute things to cuddle up with. You can't expect to hold them to your breast for a moment and not be burned. They are demonically driven by a world of darkness, invisible to our eyes, that seeks to gain your soul and pull you into the pit. That's how much Satan hates you and God.

# A TIME OF OPPORTUNITY

As I mentioned before, all eyes are being turned to God in this world right now. People around the globe are waking up to consider God. People are tuning in. People are reading their Bibles.

You might be surprised to learn that the biggest download of Christian data during the year 2020 was by the people of the nation of Iran. The gospel is going out all over the world. Billions of people are reading the Bible online.

Why? What's up? Something's happening. God has delivered this opportunity now, in an age like this, where technology can be used. We're living in a miracle right now, and I don't want you to miss "the day of your visitation," as Luke 19:44 puts it. This is an epic moment, and you will want to get on board. You want to ask God, "What do You want me to do next? Please don't do it without me."

Is that a prayer you want to pray? I do. "God, whatever You're going to do, just don't do it without me!"

Wouldn't it be a bummer if God said, "I would've loved to have used you, but you didn't recognize the day of your visitation. So I went down the street and used someone else." That's enough to break my heart.

Yes, all eyes are on God. And as we discussed in the last chapter, all eyes are off America. That may not be a popular statement, but it's true.

Listen, you can't insult the God of heaven and push Him away, and then expect Him to hang around. You can't throw Him out of colleges, throw Him out of courts, throw Him out of schools, throw Him out of the public square, throw Him out of the textbooks, and then expect Him to make our nation prosper. It's not going to happen. He's patient. He's been patient for decades, but it is very evident that our time is up.

# ISRAEL, GOD'S CHOSEN PEOPLE

The United States of America has been a stalwart friend of Israel in more ways than one for many years. And God blessed us as a nation when we stood for Israel. In fact, the prerequisite to blessing for a nation, according to the Bible, is its blessing to Israel. God says, "You bless Israel, and I will bless you."

Now, I'm not saying that everything Israel does is right. I'm not saying that just because somebody's Jewish, they are without flaw. I'm not saying that. But God makes it very clear that He will bless the nations that bless His people.

It's as if God were to walk up to you and ask you to be a friend to His friend. God asks us to be a blessing to His friend Israel, His chosen people.

"But, God," you might say, "They can be difficult people at times!" He says, "I know. That's why I chose them."

In the book of Deuteronomy, God essentially told the Israelites, "Don't think I picked you because you're better than anybody else. I picked you because you're stubborn. I picked you because you are a stiff-necked people" (see Deuteronomy 9:6). Why did He do that? To show the world that if He can save someone who is stubborn and stiff-necked, He can save you.

I love the Jewish people. They're fantastic. If you ever get into conversation with some of my Jewish friends, it's amazing because they'll argue with you for an hour. And then at the end, they'll say, "I believed everything you said. I just wanted to listen to you argue your point."

And God says, "Those argumentative, headstrong, persistently stubborn people are the ones that I'm going to pick as My chosen people. They drive everybody else up the wall, and they will be instruments of My grace and My mercy." And God picked them.

There's a reason why the Jews have historically been the most hated and persecuted people on the planet. It's because God picked them. And therefore, Satan hates them.

Think about it. God has promised an everlasting covenant with the Jewish people which He has sworn to keep. Satan knows about this covenant. And the devil thinks that if he can somehow break that covenant, if he can mess that up, then he can thwart the plan of God.

Of course, that is never going to happen.

# ISRAEL IS PROPHECY FULFILLED

We looked at Ezekiel 38 earlier in this book. Let me remind you that that prophecy is more than 2,500 years old, and yet it talks about the nation Israel as we know it today.

Why is Israel a big deal? It's the only nation in the Bible with whom God has established an everlasting covenant. Israel is special. It is the only nation in history where the Scripture foretold that they would be a nation, and then because of their rebellion against

God they would not be a nation (thrust into exile because of their disobedience), and that they would then become a nation once more.

The Bible predicted that shortly before Christ comes back, He would regather His nation from all the corners of the earth back into their own land. It's a funny thing because up until 1948, the Jewish people all over the world didn't consider that land "their own" because they had never been there before. So what did God do? He set up the country of Israel so that the Jewish people could move there.

Nobody's moving to Mars right now because it's not been set up for you to move to. In the same way, God had to set up the nation of Israel first, so that the Jewish people could "return" to it. They come home to a home where they've never been. This movement has happened, is happening, and will continue to happen.

The nation who was, then wasn't, and is again, was prophesied in Scripture. And not only have the Jews returned to the land, but they have caused it, with God's blessing, to thrive and prosper. As George Gilder, author of *The Israel Test*, states,

> *"Over the past 50 years, Israel has increased its population tenfold, its agricultural production 16-fold, and its industrial production 50-fold, while actually reducing net water consumption by 10% since 1948."*

A nation that is only the size of New Jersey is being incredibly resourceful, and God is blessing it materially.

Now, the Bible talks about the fact that tremendous trouble is coming to the nation of Israel during the Tribulation period of the last days, but that doesn't change the fact that Israel is the only nation on earth that God has an everlasting covenant agreement with.

## GOD BLESSES THOSE WHO BLESS ISRAEL

We can see through history how God has preserved and protected His people. Civilizations, nations, and empires that have tried to destroy the Jewish people include ancient Egypt, the Philistines, the Assyrian empire, the Babylonian empire, the Persian empire, the Greek empire, the Roman empire, the Byzantine empire, the Crusaders, the Spanish empire, Nazi Germany, and the Soviet Union. All of these groups have since passed into history and no longer remain.

You never go against Israel without going against the God of the Bible. You need to know that if you go against Israel, you're going to get yourself in trouble. How do we know this? In Genesis 12:1-3, God told Abraham, the father of the Jewish people,

> *"Get out of your country,*
> *From your family*
> *And from your father's house,*
> *To a land that I will show you.*
> *I will make you a great nation;*
> *I will bless you*
> *And make your name great;*
> *And you shall be a blessing.*
> *I will bless those who bless you,*
> *And I will curse him who curses you;*
> *And in you all the families of the earth shall be blessed."*

All the families of the earth shall be blessed if we bless Abraham's descendants. The Bible says that his descendants are none other than the Hebrew people. This is a verse that the Bible lays out flat. It doesn't ask you for your opinion. It doesn't apologize for it. It just says it.

You may say, "I don't think that's meant to be taken literally. It's just a poetic blessing." I would suggest you study history to see how nations and peoples fare when they go against Israel. It doesn't go well.

## GOD'S PROMISE TO ISRAEL MATTERS

Some people might think "Why should I care if all eyes are on Israel right now? How does God's fulfillment of prophecy concerning Israel affect me?"

It should affect you for this reason: it is concrete evidence that God keeps His promises. Whatever God does with Israel should excite you because God's promises to you matter. And if God doesn't keep His promises to Israel, then He is not obligated to keep His promises to you or to me.

But He will, He has, and He is keeping His promises. And that is good news for you and me as believers.

What are we to do in light of these things? These truths should energize us. Knowing that God will never fail us and never abandon us should motivate and excite us. They should also cause you and me to be bold about the truth.

Thankfully, in a world where we don't know what's true anymore, we can trust God's promises. We cannot trust an image that we see on television. We cannot trust a headline we read in the news. We cannot trust a politician or leader or government agency. We have been burned before by lies from all of those places, and in this dark and perverse generation, it is often difficult to know what's true.

Even when we go to the supposed fact-checkers, we find that they also are wrong many times. What do we do about that? We go to God's Word, which is always true. It is the steadfast immovable truth of God. It never changes. It is exactly what you need in your life. That's why Bible prophecy matters. That's why what God does with Israel matters.

God has clearly said that He loves Israel, that He loves Jerusalem, and that He has chosen the Jewish people. You want to be very careful how you approach what God says He loves. The nations of the world that have set themselves against Israel have folded and failed.

If you want to be a blessed people, a blessed nation, or even a blessed church, then bless Israel.

God is not asking you and me to turn a blind eye to every wrong thing Israel does, but God is commanding us to pray for the peace of Jerusalem and to provoke the Jewish people to love, for love of their Messiah, Jesus Christ.

## OPPOSITION TO ISRAEL

Going back to Ezekiel 38, we see that Gog, who is both a warrior and ruler who will oppose Israel in the last days, says, "I will go up against a peaceful people who dwell in safety."

You can almost see the sneer of hatred on his face. "I see those people," says Gog. "They dwell in safety. They're prospering. Look how confident they are." It infuriates him, and he is envious.

God spoke these words in Joel 3:1,

> "Behold, in those days and at that time,
> When I bring back the captives of Judah and Jerusalem,
> I will also gather all nations,
> And bring them down to the Valley of Jehoshaphat;
> And I will enter into judgment with them there
> On account of My people, My heritage Israel,
> Whom they have scattered among the nations;
> They have also divided up My land."

This prophecy was given some 2,600 years ago, and yet it sounds like we're talking about something the United Nations proposes today. "Divide the land!" they say, to appease Israel's opponents. But Zechariah 12:1-3 says,

> The Lord, who stretches out the heavens, who lays the foundation of the earth, and who forms the human spirit within a person, declares: "I am going to make Jerusalem a cup that sends all the surrounding peoples reeling. Judah will be besieged as well as Jerusalem. On that day, when all the nations of the earth are gathered against her, I will make Jerusalem an immovable rock for all the nations. All who try to move it will injure themselves." (NIV)

The Hebrew phrase for "injure themselves" means to tear up your insides from strain. It's a picture of someone who goes to pick up a rock and is so intent on picking up the rock that they rip their guts under the strain of it. You essentially tear yourself apart.

Have you ever seen Olympic weightlifters? They use every ounce of might they can to move something heavy.

The world is going to have the same mindset as an Olympic weightlifter: "We've got to deal with Jerusalem!" But they will injure themselves under the force of their attempts to do so.

What's the world's fascination with Jerusalem? There's no oil. There's no airport. There's no river. There's no skiing or other vacationing appeal. There's nothing of great value, physically, that would make it the center of attention. (Although, it does have some pretty amazing food!) Practically speaking, it makes no sense to exert so much effort in fighting over this small point on the planet.

And yet the world is doing all it can to move what God has anchored. Don't mess with Him. He's got a plan.

## WHAT THE BIBLE SAYS ABOUT ISRAEL

On May 14, 1948, Israel became a nation because American President Harry Truman went against all the deliberation and counsel of the nations of the world. Truman said, "We're going to recognize Israel as a nation.

Just one day after Bible prophecy was fulfilled and Israel once again became a nation, the headline for the *New York Times* on May 15th, 1948, read, "Zionists Proclaim New State of Israel; Truman Recognizes It and Hopes for Peace; Tel Aviv is Bombed, Egypt Orders Invasion."

Israel had no army, but they won the invasion by Egypt. How does that happen?

CHAPTER FOUR: ALL EYES ON ISRAEL

Answer: God.

Absolutely amazing.

Today, Egypt is a friend of Israel, as are Saudi Arabia and Jordan, just as the prophets foretold. It's interesting that not only are the right nations lined up to invade Israel at this moment, but the right nations, for the first time in history, are lined up to *support* Israel as well. That's not a coincidence.

Here's the amazing thing: the prophecy foretelling these things is thousands of years old. Isaiah 66:7-9 reads:

> *Before the birth pains even begin,*
> *Jerusalem gives birth to a son.*
> *Who has ever seen anything as strange as this?*
> *Who ever heard of such a thing?*
> *Has a nation ever been born in a single day?*
> *Has a country ever come forth in a mere moment?*
> *But by the time Jerusalem's birth pains begin,*
> *her children will be born.*
> *Would I ever bring this nation to the point of birth*
> *and then not deliver it?" asks the Lord.*
> *"No! I would never keep this nation from being born,"*
> *says your God.* (NLT)

Israel was first born by being called out of Egypt in the wilderness wanderings, and then eventually brought into the Promised Land by Joshua. Israel's second birth, prophesied by Isaiah, not only happened in 1948, but it happened exactly as Isaiah said it would—in a mere moment. In one day, the nation was brought forth, and instantly Jews from around the world had a nation that they could come back to.

51

The fulfillment of this one prophecy alone should dispel any doubt about the veracity of God's Word and the ability of God to keep His promises. So when He says to you, "Trust Me; I'll forgive your sins.... Look to Me.... I died on the cross for your grief and I give you eternal life... Follow Me... I'll give you purpose and meaning.... I'm the God that made you.... Trust in Me and I'll take you to heaven," you can take those promises and assurances to the bank. The God that says these things is the exact same God that kept His Word found in Isaiah 66, and who keeps His promises today.

God said in Ezekiel 34:13,

> *"I will bring them out from the peoples and gather them from the countries, and will bring them to their own land; I will feed them on the mountains of Israel, in the valleys and in all the inhabited places of the country."*

And that is exactly what God has done.

# CHAPTER
## FIVE

---∾◦∾---

## All Eyes to War

Regarding the nation of Israel, the past, present, and future have been written. We know what happened to them. We know what's happening to them. And we know from the Bible what's going to happen to them.

But as I stated before, America is nowhere mentioned in the Bible. That brings me great pain and it brings me great hope. It pains me because our nation was very much used as a big brother to Israel's reestablishment. America is a Judeo-Christian nation in its roots. This nation has been blessed in every category, over every nation on earth and in all of human history. America has had the freest people, the freest constitutional government, the greatest technologies, the greatest military, the greatest achievements, and more.

America has also been the most compassionate nation on the face of the earth. No nation—and no nation's citizens—give more to disaster relief and suffering than the United States. Year after year, God used this nation to benefit others. At one time, the annual federal budget of the United States government included funds to produce Bibles and ship them to nations in the world where there were no Bibles. When soldiers went off to war in World War I, World War II, and the Korean War, they were given Bibles. I have one myself.

"Oh, how the mighty have fallen," says the Scripture. That lament can certainly be said of America.

Where do we go from here? God is not waiting on any political party, or for a brilliant chess-like move by some political genius, or for some international blunder to happen, in order to move. God is saying,

*"If My people who are called by My name will humble themselves, and pray and seek My face, and turn from their wicked ways, then I will hear from heaven, and will forgive their sin and heal their land."* (2 Chronicles 7:14)

"I will move," says the Lord, "if My people will call out to Me and repent."

Why is everything in limbo? Why is everything so undetermined and perplexing? There's nothing but confusion all around us, especially in light of the many recent months of global panic and misinformation and chaos. It has been the most bizarre time ever... and yet all around the world, record numbers of people are coming to Christ.

What's up for America? Well, I'm no Einstein, but I can tell you this based on God's Word. There's no hope for America unless:

1) The Church stops playing games, stops goofing off, and starts teaching the Bible and living in obedience to God's Word—and I mean from the pulpit to the pew.

2) Real changes are made in individual homes. A nation goes as a home goes. But a home doesn't know how to change unless the Church steps up and teaches God's Word. That's true in the Bible, it's true in sociology studies, and it's true in American history. When churches catch fire and come alive with the power of the Spirit and the message of the gospel, that affects families. Drunks stop drinking, abusers stop abusing, cheaters stop cheating— and they begin to make their home work like it should.

And from there, the community changes, and then the county changes, the state changes, and the nation changes. That's the only hope for America—revival that starts in individuals and homes. But the Church has to step up and be the salt and light that is called to be.

God is not going to sprinkle pixie dust over America and make it magically soar. He is going to be true to His pattern. Again:

> *"If My people who are called by My name will humble themselves, and pray and seek My face, and turn from their wicked ways, then I will hear from heaven, and will forgive their sin and heal their land."*

That's the only hope for America. If that doesn't happen, it's all over. And God's showing us little hints and glimpses of what it's like when He's left the building. This is a very critical time and it's going to lead to war.

Everyone knows that on the playground, the bully takes advantage of the weak kid. If you want to stop a bully, you teach the other kids how to defend themselves. The issue of bullying starts in the heart. You can make rules to try to stop a bully, but that's never going to change the heart. Until hearts are changed, your kid's got to be able to protect himself against the bully. Bullies find the weak because bullies are cowards.

So how does that apply to nations? There are a lot of coward nations out there right now who want to pick a fight. Many of them are led by lunatics. They've got nuclear weapons and an itching trigger finger and they don't know what to do, but they feel like they should do something. They want to feel powerful. The United Nations can do its best to legislate rules and sanctions and mandates, but it's no good unless someone stands in opposition to the bully. That someone used to be the United States, but not anymore. The bully nations are threatening and positioning for war.

# SIGNS OF THE END TIMES

Jesus said in Matthew 24:6,

> *You will hear of wars and rumors of wars. See that you are not troubled; for all these things must come to pass, but the end is not yet.*

In that same chapter, Jesus predicted that there would be pandemics. Does that surprise you? The term He uses for global sickness is "pestilences." Jesus also said there's going to be lawlessness—a complete disregard for the laws of both God and men.

But these things were not the first things Jesus told His disciples to look for when they came to Him and asked,

> *"Tell us, when will these things be? And what will be the sign of Your coming, and of the end of the age?"*
> (Matthew 24:3)

Jesus did not say first that there are going to be wars and rumors of wars, or that there are going to be earthquakes, or that there would be famines. Those were all things He mentioned later in His answer, but they are not what He said first.

Jesus also said that men will hate one another so much that their love will grow cold for humanity. And because of that, lawlessness will prevail. Nobody will fear the law and people will do what is right in their own eyes. But He didn't say any of that first, either.

Here is what Jesus said first. He said,

> *"Take heed that no one deceives you. For many will come in My name, saying, 'I am the Christ,' and will deceive many."* (Matthew 24:4-5)

There will be deception. How extreme will the deception be? Jesus said in Matthew 24:24 that

> *"There shall arise false Christs, and false prophets, and shall show great signs and wonders; insomuch that, if it were possible, they shall deceive the very elect."* (KJV)

He didn't say the elect are going to be deceived. He said the opposite. "If it were possible..." That means it's impossible. You don't need a logic course to understand that if something's not possible, then it's impossible.

How is it impossible for the elect to be deceived? Because when the Word of God is in you, it keeps you from being deceived by the dark world around you.

## GOD'S GOT YOU COVERED

God is so gracious with you in your spiritual journey, whether you are just starting out or you're a seasoned saint. He sustains you throughout. But to whom much is given, from him much will be required (see Luke 12:48). As you grow older in Jesus, you depend on faith more than feelings. When you're a new believer, it's all feelings and a little bit of faith, but

> *"Faith comes by hearing, and hearing by the word of God"* (Romans 10:17).

I love being around new believers. They're awesome. They're expressive of their love for Jesus and just want to praise Him and talk about Him. Maybe they'll say something like, "I'm going to pray because I don't have a job." And they pray, "Lord, I need a job. I'd like to have a good one. Thank You, Jesus. Amen." And you think, "That's nice."

And then they call you the next day: "Hey, I got a phone call. Some company called me up and offered me a job, and it pays really well. Praise the Lord!"

With new believers, it seems wherever they go, they pray and God just goes, "Boom. There you go. Prayer answered." Hang out with new believers and you'll see what I mean. They will say something like, "I just sense the Lord right now," and a seasoned saint right next to them is thinking, "I don't sense anything. What are you sensing?"

The thing is, God is working in the journey at different levels with His grace. And where there's more of the Word, God moves you from feelings to faith in the things He has written there. In time you learn more of the Word, so that you will know it and depend on it and trust in it when you need it. And in those faith-building seasons, you learn that God keeps His Word.

So the new believers are covered and the seasoned saints are covered because God is faithful.

My friend, it doesn't matter if you are a brand-new believer who is just starting your walk with Jesus, or you're an old, seasoned saint who has walked with God for a long time. I want to encourage you that God's prophetic promise in His Bible is to bring you peace. Jesus talked about how knowing the future brings comfort for the believer. Paul the apostle said the same thing. And the same sentiment was echoed from the mouth of Peter as well. Bible prophecy should comfort us. In fact, the first and the greatest Bible prophecy of all Scripture is in Genesis 3. There God promised us salvation through the Messiah who would crush the devil's head. That promised Messiah is Jesus Christ.

# AN
# INVITATION

Maybe you are neither a new believer nor a seasoned saint, and you're starting to realize that you need to walk with Jesus. If that's you, please understand that Jesus Christ died for your sins and mine. He died on the cross. It wasn't an accident, and it wasn't an incident. It was according to the prophetic word of God. It was prophesied that Christ would be born in Bethlehem of a virgin, die a brutal death, and be resurrected from the dead in order that you could be made right before God. And by trusting in what Christ has done, you can have eternal life.

If you would like to pray a prayer asking God to save you from the punishment of your sins—if you would like to begin a loving relationship with the One who made you, you can pray a prayer like this:

*"Dear God, I ask You to forgive me of my sins. I ask You to wash me clean in the blood of the Lamb of God, Jesus Christ. Lord, I confess today that You died for me and that You rose again from the dead. And I choose, of my own will, the decision for Jesus to be my Lord and Savior. In His name I pray. Amen."*

If you've prayed that prayer, we would love to give you a free Bible and resources to help you grow in your faith. Please reach out to us by simply going to JackHibbs.com and letting us know that you made a decision for Jesus Christ. I'd love to send you a free Bible so that you can read for yourself what it has to say about what God is like, what will happen in the end times, and how you should live today.

# CHAPTER
## SIX

‹‹‹‹‹‹‹‹‹›‹·‹›‹›‹›‹›‹›

## So, What's Next?

There's no doubt about it: in today's world, instability is everywhere.

The great thing is that we as believers do not have to feel unstable, because the truth of God's Word is sure and steadfast.

So what's next for us as Christians? What's the next prophetic event for the Church to look for?

The Bible's very clear that at any moment, Jesus could come back for the Church. We call this event the Rapture.

As of right now, there is nothing that stands in the way of the Rapture being the next major event on the end-times calendar to occur.

## WHAT IS THE RAPTURE?

The English word *rapture* doesn't actually appear in the Bible. Some people use that as a reason to not believe that the Rapture will happen. But while the English word is not there, the doctrine is. If you were to read the Bible in Latin you would see it as *rapturo*. The word *rapture* in Greek is *harpazo*. In English, it's translated as "caught up."

It means to be snatched away, forcibly removed. But it's not a bad removal. It's like being pulled from a train track to safety because of an oncoming train. *Harpazo* = Rapture = caught up.

I am going to give you five passages about the Rapture from each of the five chapters of 1 Thessalonians.

When Paul preached in Thessalonica, scholars agree that he was there somewhere between three to four weeks. That's it! Before he came, there were no Christians. Then Paul preached, and pagans began to accept Christ. He set up a church and he moved on. Sometime later, he writes them a letter because he heard that they were panicking. They thought that they had somehow missed the last-days events. So Paul wrote this letter to reassure them.

## PASSAGE #1 – 1 THESSALONIANS 1:10

Here's the first verse:

> Wait for [God's] Son from heaven, whom He raised from the dead, even Jesus who delivers us from the wrath to come.

Do you see the word *wrath*? This is not talking about hell. This word has nothing to do with hell, but has everything to do with God's wrath that's going to be poured out upon the earth for a Christ-rejecting world.

The Thessalonian Christians were afraid that they had missed Jesus' appearing and that they were going to have to go through the wrathful judgment of God. But Paul assures them in his letter.

"Paul, did we miss it?"

"No, you didn't miss it. Keep looking, keep watching."

## PASSAGE #2 – 1 THESSALONIANS 2:19

> For what is our hope, or joy, or crown of rejoicing? Is it not even you in the presence of our Lord Jesus Christ at His coming?

Reassuring them again, Paul tells the Thessalonians that they will be present at the Lord's return.

## PASSAGE #3 – 1 THESSALONIANS 3:13

> *So that He may establish your hearts blameless in holiness before our God and Father at the coming of our Lord Jesus Christ with all His saints.*

"*All His saints*" includes those believers who have preceded us in death. We'll talk more about that in just a bit.

## PASSAGE #4 – 1 THESSALONIANS 4:13-18

We will break this passage up a bit. 1 Thessalonians 4:13 says:

> *But I do not want you to be ignorant, brethren, concerning those who have fallen asleep, lest you sorrow as others who have no hope. For if we believe that Jesus died and rose again, even so God will bring with Him those who sleep in Jesus.*

Paul uses the word *sleep* when he talks about death to remind the Thessalonians that their death is not permanent. This sleep refers to their bodies, not their souls. There is no such thing in the Bible as "soul sleep." Some cults will teach that when you die, your soul is in some sort of unconscious state and then someday you will wake up again. But the Bible doesn't teach that. It says that "*to be absent from the body*" is "*to be present with the Lord*" (see 2 Corinthians 5:8).

Paul prefaced the next part of this passage with these words.

*For this we say to you by the word of the Lord...* (Verse 15)

In other words, Paul is saying, "This is not my promise. This is the Lord's promise."

I don't like promises unless Jesus gives them. Promises that people give used to get me excited. Now I'd rather not hear them. People break their promises. But Jesus is the Promise-keeper. What does God promise?

> *That we who are alive and remain until the coming of the Lord will by no means precede those who are asleep. For the Lord Himself will descend from heaven with a shout, with the voice of an archangel, and with the trumpet of God. And the dead in Christ will rise first.* (Verses 15-16)

One of the great attributes of a new toaster with brand-new springs is its popping action. When you put the bread in and you make toast for the first time, you'd better be ready. When that thing's done, that toast comes shooting out of that toaster so fast you can't even grab it. According to the Bible, we will hear that voice and that trumpet and—boom!—the bodies of the dead in Christ will pop up out of their graves. Forest Lawn Cemetery is going to look like a mega-toaster filled with Pop-Tarts coming up out of it. Amazing.

The Bible then says that

> *We who are alive and remain shall be caught up* [the word *Rapture*] *together with them in the clouds to meet the Lord in the air. And thus we shall always be with the Lord.* (Verses 17-18)

Notice the specific words, "in the clouds" and "in the air." This is not an ethereal, cosmic, magical kind of concept. Paul used an atmospheric designation. Scientifically speaking, the atmosphere covers anything from zero elevation to about 126,000 feet. The Bible says we are someday going to meet Jesus in the atmospheric sky. Can you just imagine the view?

We will meet the Lord in the air. "And thus, we shall always be with the Lord." Isn't that what you're living for? To be with Him?

> *Therefore comfort one another with these words.*
> (Verse 18)

That certainly is a great comfort. That is going to be a good day. No wonder the Bible calls it "the blessed hope." But, let's be honest. If you're a Christian, but you're disobeying God's commands, this probably doesn't sound so exciting to you.

Maybe you are sleeping around and God has been saying to you, "You ought not to be doing this." Or maybe you're getting back into dabbling in the world of drugs, and Jesus is saying, "Come on, get out of that. We don't do that anymore." Or perhaps you're snooping around pornography sites and looking at things you ought not to be looking at, and the Holy Spirit says, "You belong to Me now; stop it."

If that is you, then the thought of Christ's return—which is something that ought to be very comforting—becomes something uncomfortable. The glorious appearing of Jesus becomes something stressful for the Christian who's not walking right with God.

I might say to a fellow believer, "Oh man, I hope the Lord comes back today!" And if they're obviously less than excited about the prospect, I know there's something going on. The Christian who is not walking with God doesn't like to hear about Jesus coming back. But it's exactly what they need to hear. Jesus could come back at any time, and that should be a source of hope, not panic.

But if you're not a Christian, you might as well just panic right now, because if you truly understood that you are one breath away from an eternity in hell, you'd say, "I need to accept God's gift of salvation before something happens to me!" And you would be right.

# PASSAGE #5 – 1 THESSALONIANS 5:9

Our final verse from 1 Thessalonians says,

> For God did not appoint us to wrath [His vengeance that's coming upon the earth], but to obtain salvation through our Lord Jesus Christ.

That's great news, isn't it? God's people are not destined for wrath, but for salvation. And it's all because of the sacrifice of Jesus on the cross.

Here are some key points to remember when we talk about the Rapture.

# THE RAPTURE IS A PROMISED EVENT

The Rapture is promised to us by none other than Jesus Christ Himself in John 14:1-3.

> Let not your heart be troubled; you believe in God, believe also in Me. In My Father's house are many mansions; if it

*were not so, I would have told you. I go to prepare a place for you. And if I go and prepare a place for you, I will come again and receive you to Myself; that where I am, there you may be also.*

Jesus left earth 2,000 years ago and He said, "I'm going to go away and I'm going to prepare a place for you." Just think about the fact that He created the entire universe in six days, but He's been preparing a place for us for nearly 2,000 years. I think it's going to be pretty amazing.

What is He going to do after He prepares a place for us?

*I will come again and receive you to Myself; that where I am, there you may be also.*

Jesus very clearly tells His people that He's coming to get us and will bring us to the place He has prepared for us.

How do we get there? What is the vehicle? The Rapture. We will be "caught up," off of this globe and out of this world. He will collect both the living and the dead who are His in the atmosphere. And from there He will take us into His presence in heaven, away from all that will happen on earth. That is thrilling news.

Jesus promises to descend from heaven, raise the dead in Christ, and catch us up together with Him in the air. And then He promises that we shall always be with the Lord. Hallelujah! The Rapture of the Church is a promised event!

# THE RAPTURE IS A SUDDEN EVENT

Imagine an umbrella. I'm holding the handle and the umbrella's over my head. Under the umbrella, from one edge to the handle, is the Rapture. And on the other side, from the handle to the other edge, is the Second Coming. On the outside of the umbrella, over the ribbing, it says "The Second Coming of Christ."

Collectively, it's called the Second Coming. But the Second Coming is broken up into two manifestations: one is the appearance of Jesus in the atmosphere, and the other is the physical return of Jesus on the earth, specifically in Jerusalem.

That's why Jerusalem's always in the news. That's why everybody fights over Jerusalem. As I stated before, there is nothing physically of great value to draw people to desire Jerusalem. It's a spiritual issue. It's the place about which God says, "This is where My name dwells."

The ancient Hebrew scholars believe that when God spoke the physical universe into existence, Jerusalem was under His feet when it formed. I can't confirm if that's true because I wasn't there, but God says, "I love Jerusalem."

And one day, He will return and physically touch down to earth there. But the Rapture happens separately from that event, and it is sudden. There is no prophetic precursors or requirements for the Rapture to take place. It is imminent, and it will be without warning.

There are nearly 280 prophecies that have to be fulfilled before the Second Coming can take place. But there are no unfulfilled prophecies standing in the way of the Rapture.

When Jesus comes at the Rapture, He comes to collect those that believe in Him from all around the globe, both the living and the dead. When He comes back at the Second Coming, it's specifically to finish His covenant promises that were given to Israel regarding their relationship with Him.

The Rapture will happen in the twinkling of an eye. It's a sudden event.

Paul believed that he would be among those who would be raptured. You can tell because he used the pronoun *we*: *We* who are alive and remain.... *We* shall be caught up.... Thus *we* shall always be with the Lord

Paul didn't give up that idea until 2 Timothy 4, when he conceded,

> The time of my departure is at hand. I have fought the good fight, I have finished the race, I have kept the faith. (Verses 6-7)

Every generation of believers, from the time of the early Church until now, has expected the imminent return of Christ in their lifetime. Even the disciples believed Christ would return before they died. Isn't that interesting? You might say to me, "My grandmother said Jesus was coming back." Well, that means your grandmother was ready. Are you? If your grandmother said it and believed it, how much closer are we to that blessed hope today?

Just because people have been saying it for centuries, it doesn't mean it's not going to happen. It means we're that much closer. It's going to happen.

How can I be so sure? Because God said it's going to happen, and God always keeps His word.

We read in 1 Corinthians 15:51-52,

> *Behold, I tell you a mystery: We shall not all sleep, but we shall all be changed—in a moment, in the twinkling of an eye, at the last trumpet. For the trumpet will sound, and the dead will be raised incorruptible, and we shall be changed.*

The word *mystery* in Greek is *mysterion*. It means something that has always existed, always been there, always been true, but there's been no reason to unveil it yet. Paul is saying that there was no reason for the *mysterion* he's about to mention to be given in the Old Testament. It's God's eternal truth, but it had been veiled until needed. But now, in the Church age, the mystery is revealed because Church-age believers need to be ready to meet Christ.

Paul says that *"we shall not all sleep."* That refers to the death of the physical body, not the soul, as I mentioned before.

How long will it take for us to be changed? *"In the twinkling of an eye."* Experts argue whether that's 18 thousandths of a second or 22 thousandths of a second. Who cares? It's fast!

Paul says that this will happen, *"at the last trumpet. For the trumpet will sound, and the dead will be raised incorruptible, and we shall be changed."* What does that *"last trumpet"* refer to?

Some people see "last trumpet" and think that this has to be part of the seven trumpet judgments found in the book of Revelation. From there they assume the Rapture has to be at the end of the Tribulation period. But this trumpet has nothing to do with that.

The whole context of this trumpet is referring to the gathering together of God's people. In chapter 10 of the book of Numbers,

God told Moses to make two trumpets out of silver that were to be used for the calling together of the congregation. When one trumpet was blown, the leaders of Israel would be summoned. But when both trumpets were blown—the first trumpet and the last trumpet—God was calling together the entire assembly of the people.

One trumpet = an incomplete gathering. Two trumpets = everyone assembles. At the Rapture, the *entire* assembly of Church-age believers are being summoned—both the dead in Christ and we who are alive and remain.

The dead will be raised incorruptible (not as decaying zombies from a horror film, but incorruptible—not capable of deteriorating), and we, the saints who are still alive, shall be transformed, metamorphosed, molecularly transfigured. Isn't that amazing to think about?

## THE RAPTURE IS A REQUIRED EVENT

The Rapture is not only something exciting, but it has to happen as part of God's redemptive process. In 2 Peter 3:3-4, Peter warned

> ...that scoffers will come in the last days, walking according to their own lusts, and saying, "Where is the promise of His coming? For since the fathers fell asleep, all things continue as they were from the beginning of creation."

This is happening today. People are scoffing at the idea of the return of Christ. And ironically, in doing so they are fulfilling this very verse and giving credence to what has been prophesied in the Bible.

Those who mock are just one more evidence of the soon return of Jesus Christ. And the closer we get to His coming, there will be more and more people not believing it. There will be more and more people departing from the faith. There will be more and more people rejecting the truth. That's just one more of the indicators to look for in the last days.

This increased rejection of God's truth in the last days can cause some of us to worry. But let's go back to the reassuring words of Jesus when He said,

> *Let not your heart be troubled; you believe in God, believe also in Me... And if I go and prepare a place for you, I will come again and receive you to Myself; that where I am, there you may be also. (John 14:1,3)*

God's word is certain. Don't let anyone tell you otherwise. God will fulfill His prophetic word. He always has. And what's left for Him to fulfill, He will do. You can count on Him.

Jesus could come back this year, this month, or even this very day. I pray He comes soon. And until that day, I encourage you to stay in the Word of God, be watching, waiting, and working to bring others to Him in these remarkable days.